Binding the Spirit of Fear, Worry and Depression.

Divine Revelations and Powerful Prayers to Bind and Cast Out Fear, Worry and Depression from Your Life Permanently.

DANIEL C. OKPARA

Disclaimer

The information presented herein represents the views of the author as of the date of publication. Because of the rate with which conditions change, the author reserves the rights to alter and update his opinions based on the new conditions. This product is for edification purposes only and the author does not accept any responsibilities for any liabilities resulting from the use of this information.

While every attempt has been made to verify the information provided here, the author and referrals cannot assume any responsibility for errors, inaccuracies or omissions. Any slights of people or organizations are unintentional.

Copyright © September 2016 by Daniel C. Okpara

All Rights Reserved. Contents of this book may not be reproduced in any way or by any means without written consent of the publisher, with exception of brief excerpts in critical reviews and articles.

Published By:
Better Life Media.
BETTER LIFE WORLD OUTREACH CENTER.
Website: www.BetterLifeWorld.org
Email: info@betterlifeworld.org

Any scripture quotation in this book is taken from the King James Version of the Bible except where stated. Used by permission.

All texts, calls, letters, testimonies and enquiries are welcome.

Contents.

Introduction..10

Chapter 1: Why That Woman Died Instantly........................13

Chapter 2: The Power of Your Enemy is Your Fear of What He Can Do..17

Chapter 3: The Secret Behind the Power of Goliath and Jezebel..28

Chapter 4: The 5 Dangerous Fruits of Fear and Worry...36

Chapter 5: The 11 Types of Fear to Deal With......43

Chapter 6: Strategies to Defeat Fear, Worry and Depression Permanently..68

Chapter 7: 45 Powerful Prayers & Declarations to Cast Out Fear, Worry, Depression and Panic Attacks Forever............75

Resources from Better Life World Outreach Center.............92

Connect With Us...94

About the Author..96

Introduction.

Fear, worry and depression are three powerful tools the devil can use to hold you down and cause serious troubles in your life and family for a long time. These tools are used by the devil to torment and harass people unnecessarily.

For instance, if the devil can get you to be worried or afraid of what tomorrow holds, he will subsequently attack your body with some ailments. If he can get you to be afraid of losing your money in investments, he will attack you with financial crisis eventually. If he can get you to be afraid that you'll lose your job, he'll cause you to do things that will make you lose your job, go broke and query the goodness of God.

Every time we allow fear, worry and depression to get hold of us, we sow seeds that will likely grow into pains, losses and other problems.

John the Baptist was a mighty man of God. In fact, Jesus said that of all men born, there was none as great as John the Baptist. But he died like a chicken, with his head severed and presented on a platter at the request of a dancer. The entire powers of heaven at his disposal were silent, while he died like an ordinary servant. Why? Because he got worried, became depressed and doubted the ONE he knew very well and earlier confessed.

In this book the LORD has asked me to show you the strategies the enemy uses to get you to worry, fear and get depressed. And then stand in God's authority given to you and **bind and cast these spirits out** and reclaim your peace and confidence.

KEEP THE DEVIL IN HIS PROPER PLACE

While praying some time ago, the LORD gave me a strong Word. He spoke to my heart and said, *"Satan has no power over you except the one you give him."*

That WORD has helped me to appreciate the place of Satan properly and keep him where he is supposed to be. Yes. Satan's best place is **UNDER MY FEET.** That's his best place to be, and I don't intend to change my understanding any time soon.

I strongly believe that Satan is always where we put him in our lives, families and endeavours. I believe that Satan is even surprised with the kind of attention we give him. He feels like, *"wow, I must be some kind of a pop star. These dudes call me constantly every day."*

Today, I want to challenge you to reappoint the devil and keep him where he performs better; and that is UNDER YOUR FEET. I want to give you tools and strategies for dealing with the powers of darkness and living a victorious life in Christ Jesus.

If you imbibe the few thoughts and ideas the LORD is laying in my heart to bring across to you through this book, you'll find your fears, worries and concerns trashed before you know it. You'll discover that Satan's greatest weapon is within your control. And as long as you learn to handle him, you'll see yourself living a victorious life every day.

Chapter 1: Why That Woman Died Instantly.

I was told a story that touched my heart greatly by one of our precious sisters in church some time ago. The incident happened in the small town from where I originally wrote this book, where I also happened to be a pastor of a church.

As I was told, a group of women had boarded a pick-up truck to go sell their goods in one of their regular village markets. On the way, the vehicle suddenly lost its brakes while on a very high speed. As usual, terror and uproar immediately set in among the passengers. It was, "hei...hei...hei...Jesus! Jesus! Jesus!" etc.

But that didn't stop the vehicle from its *death-bent race.* In the process, one of the passengers jumped out, hoping to escape from the impending judgement the vehicle was headed. Unfortunately, that turned out to be a wrong call. She was smashed beyond repair and died on the spot.

Others, though very terrified and confused, did not follow her example. Did any one of them at that moment think that step didn't pay, or was it just a matter of sheer luck that they didn't consider jumping out like the other woman did? Or did any of them remember that **the first thing to do when you don't know what to do is to do nothing?** Or was it just a coincidence that more of them didn't express their fear by joining that poor woman to jump out of the moving vehicle?

As I was told, the vehicle somehow miraculously stopped from the rough, death race. And the other passengers came out with very minor injuries. But they had lost one soul, the precious woman who jumped out.

Her colleagues in the small pick-up truck was said to sustain minor wounds. They did not have to get admitted in the hospital to get those wounds healed. But the other woman had died.

Only she…….why?

Most times, it's not fair to use matters that concern loss of life for illustration in teachings because no matter what you try to say, the lost life cannot come back. But then, like you, I've asked a lot of questions in events like that.

Why was this woman the only person who died in that accident? Was it her destiny or an act of God?

WHAT DO YOU DO WHEN FACED WITH DANGER?

Many of us react differently during times of danger. And rightly so, we are not to blame ourselves for what we do at such times. However, there are a few tips that might help us in advance to handle danger moments:

1. The best thing to do when you don't know what to do is to do nothing.
2. We can drastically reduce the potency of a dangerous situation we find ourselves with how we handle ourselves at such times.
3. Whatever we do out of fear doesn't usually have a good ending.
4. Even when you are obviously scared to the teeth, initially pretending like you're okay will

give you some edge in deciding the best way to respond to what is before you.

I agree that when we find ourselves in danger moments, it's usually difficult to calculate our responses properly. But statistics has shown that more damage is caused by our reactions to danger than the danger itself.

The beloved woman in our story was not destined to die, neither was it God who killed her. I believe (note: this is my conviction) she died because ***she acted FEAR.***

I believe that Satan's greatest weapons are FEAR, WORRY AND DEPRESSION. I believe the devil has succeeded in causing a lot of havoc in homes and societies because of fear and worry.

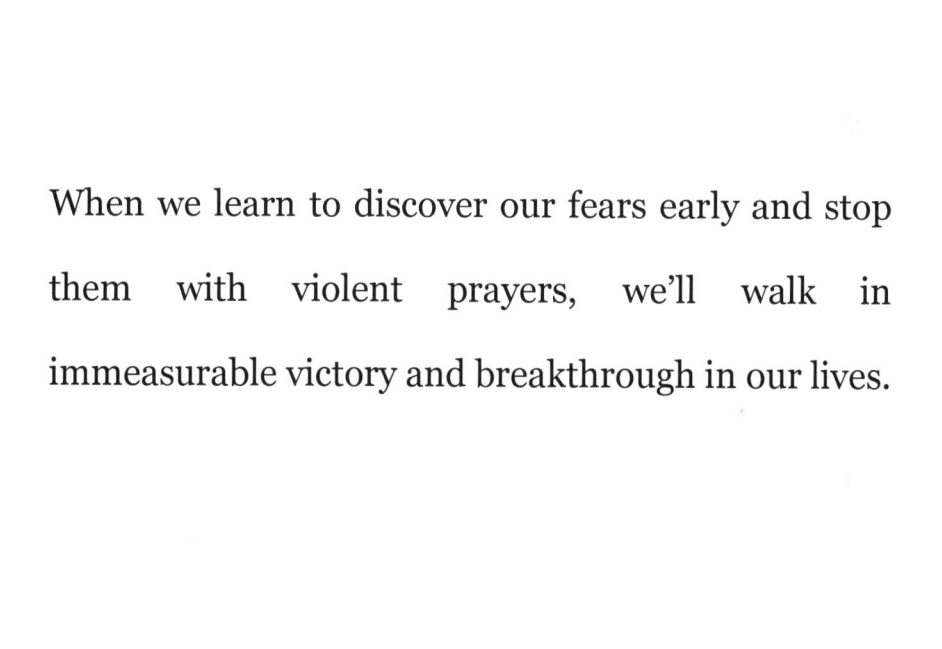

When we learn to discover our fears early and stop them with violent prayers, we'll walk in immeasurable victory and breakthrough in our lives.

Chapter 2: **The Power of Your Enemy is Your Fear of What He Can Do.**

Is there a thing you fear about most in your life?

I got bad news for you.

It's true that many times what we fear and worry about are only in our heads. Most times they are not real. But the Bible also paints a clear picture that many times our fears and worries bring those consequences closer to our lives.

Our fears and worries give life to consequences that do not exist and command them to take shape and come and deal with us. Your fear is bringing that consequence closer to your life on a daily basis than you think.

While faith is the greatest force behind any victory

in life, fear is the greatest force behind any defeat in life

EXAMPLE 1: THE FALL OF JERICO

Rehab, the harlot from Jericho confessed:

I know that the lord has given this land to you and that a great fear of you has fallen on us so that all who live in the country are melting in fear because of you - Joshua 2:8

That great city of Jericho had already been defeated even before the Israelites stepped on its shores. God had already sent fear and terror on the whole land of Jericho. They had lost the battle even before it was fought. That is God's plan in Exodus 23:27:

"I will send my terror ahead of you and throw into confusion every nation you encounter. I will make all your enemies

turn their back and run."

God is simply saying that He would use the weapon of fear to subdue their enemies before their face.

God uses the weapon of fear on our enemies. He sends fear of our capabilities ahead of us and our enemies are subdued. Unfortunately, our enemies also try to use the weapon of fear on us. Any side that gets afraid loses the battle even before it is fought.

Whatever battle you confront with fear, you have already lost it. But with faith, you have already won even before fighting.

By the way, notice how the people of Jericho contracted this fear that made them lose even before fighting. Rehab said:

*We have **HEARD** how the Lord dried up the water of the Red Sea for you when you came out of Egypt, and what you did to Sihon and Og, the two kings of the Amorites east of the Jordan, whom you completely destroyed*

***WHEN WE HEARD** of it, our hearts melted in fear and everyone's courage failed because of you, for the Lord your God is God in heaven above and on the earth below* - Joshua 2:9-11.

Note the bolded words. The people of Jericho got their fear from the NEWS they heard, and so lost, even without fighting. Of course, the fall of Jericho was part of God's plan for the lives of the Israelites, so that was a good outcome from our perspective. But there's some lesson to learn there as well.

The enemy is afflicting God's people with fear from

WHAT THEY HEAR. Right from the news on TV, to news about witches, wizards, terrorists, occult men, etc. We become afraid and so lose our victory even before a fight takes place.

The truth is that the first cure for fear is to *guard what you allow yourself to listen to*. I've found out that the news has a way of making us get annoyed and even afraid sometimes. Unfortunately, this innate fear weakens our victory gear in the face of life. We must learn to take the news with Faith, because as God's children, our words and thoughts are not to be decided by the news and stories that fly around, but by what God has said about us.

"The economy is very bad."

"That sickness has killed so, so and so"

"People don't do well in that place"

"That area is very dangerous at nights"

Etc!

These statements and their likes may seem to be facts as they appear to be, but they are not what God is saying about your life. They only enslave you to fear and deprive you of your rights in God if you ponder over them.

For example, never ever believe you are suffering from an incurable disease. That an expert with forty years of experience said so does not make it true. He has only done his best and doesn't know what to do next. Discover God's verdict before you conclude! Even if that expert has the facts, there could be other ways to manage the situation and further your life.

EXAMPLE 2: JOB – FROM RICHES TO RAGS

Just like you, I've read the story of Job so many times and often wondered why God would allow such evil to befall someone who "feared" him and walked righteously. I remember assuming from that story that poverty, misery, afflictions, happiness and wealth were all acts of God and that we have no say other than to accept what God decides. He might decide I get a good chunk out of life, while the other fellow gets the left overs. No questions.

The truth is that it's not all up to God. We've got a say in the entire process of realizing God's plans for our lives. The scriptures say:

"And ye shall serve the Lord your God, and he shall bless thy bread, and thy water; and I will take

sickness away from the midst of thee.

"There shall nothing cast their young, nor be barren, in thy land: the number of thy days I will fulfil.

"I will send my fear before thee, and will destroy all the people to whom thou shalt come, and I will make all thine enemies turn their backs unto thee" - Exodus 23:25-27

I believe that it was because Job was serving God that he became the richest man in the whole of the eastern part of the world at that time. So why then did God allow such evil to suddenly visit him? Why did sickness, death and loss suddenly visit a man for whom it is written, *"he feared God and shunned evil"* (Job 1-1).

The Bible says that *"the path of the just is as shining light, that shine brighter and brighter until the perfect day"* (Proverbs 4:18). This doesn't mean we won't have challenges and obstacles. But it means that that the challenges and obstacles will not swallow us up. In the challenges, we'll always come out victorious.

Yes, Job came out victorious. But I believe that the fall from riches to rags was an act of the devil. The question is why did that attack take place? Why did Job have to fall from riches to rags suddenly - when he is recorded to be a just and blameless man and was supposed to wax stronger and stronger?

There's certainly a loophole somewhere! We have only preached the other side to encourage people to exercise patience when they are tested; but we fail to state clearly that Job wasn't actually supposed to be a victim of the attacks he had from the devil.

I strongly believe it was the loophole that became a doorway for whatever he had to go through. Here's what he said himself:

> *What I feared has come upon me; what I dreaded has happened to me* - **Job 3:25.**

This statement seemed to mean that Job was serving God in fear, not the reverent fear of worship, but a fear that if he doesn't serve God that he would lose his wealth and suffer. He seemed to see God as ONE who was always waiting for someone to make a mistake so He could punish him.

He never fully trusted God to preserve him always. All his sacrifices and acts of holiness were filled with… *"I just have to do this; else, if i make a mistake, sure, God might destroy my wealth"*

He was always afraid of disaster and failure. It was this constant fear that eventually opened the door for the devil to strike.

I believe the story of Job's loss has more to teach us about the power of fear and partial belief, in addition to the other things we've taught from it. I believe that **Job's fears were what opened the door for Satan to strike his wealth.**

TO SERVE GOD EFFECTIVELY, WE ARE COMMANDED TO FEAR NOT.

If you read the bible very well you'll discover that "FEAR NOT "is one of the instructions one is required to fulfill in order to continually enjoy God's blessings. For example, when God wanted to bless

Hagar and Ishmael, her son, she was commanded to FEAR NOT (Gen. 12:17). When God wanted to restate His covenant with Abraham to Isaac, He commanded Isaac to FEAR NOT (Gen 26:24).

What about Joshua, David, Gideon, Jacob, Samuel, Hannah, Mary, Elisabeth, and the apostles? One of the instructions they were given to fulfil in order to walk in God's covenant was FEAR NOT.

Fear disqualifies us from walking with God. It opens the door for evil spirits to attack us and cause other problems. It is the biggest weapon the enemy uses against us.

In fact, fear is so bad that the Bible puts the "FEARFUL" in the same category with adulterers, whoremongers, idolaters and murderers (See Rev. 21:8)

I perceive that God allowed Job to get some discipline so that, among other reasons, fear could be uprooted from his life.

What I feared has come upon me; what I dreaded has happened to me - **Job 3:25.**

That is a very revealing statement. One who allowed such fear to dwell in him, I'm still wondering, how he could be said to fully trust God.

WHAT YOU FEAR, YOU ATTRACT FASTER IN YOUR LIFE.

For example, if you allow the fear of death to dominate your thought, God has nothing to do than to allow you die quickly. The fear of death does not stop death. It rather gives power to death to come quicker.

If you are always afraid that you may lose your job

or wealth, sorry, you may lose it sooner than you thought.... because that fear will make you unconsciously begin to do things that will now make you lose it.

What I feared has come upon me; what I dreaded has happened to me - **Job 3:25.**

Recently, a sister told me, "I'm afraid that when I get to school (she was working toward her university education) whether I'll hold onto my faith. There are lots of corruptions in the campus." She went on to tell me certain specific things she was afraid off.

"Well", I said, "many people have not lost their faith on campus, so why will you? You are creating your own problems by the thought and fear which you are nurturing in your mind."

I showed her Isaiah 45:2 where God said, "I will go

before you and make the crooked places straight, I will break down the gates of bronze and cut through bars of iron.

I showed her that the "ways of a righteous man (of course, that doesn't mean a perfect man) is ordered by the LORD" (Psalm 37:23) and that "your going out and coming in will be a blessing and not a curse (Psalm 121:8)

By the time I was through with those few verses, she was all joy. Her face lit up and she realized that her negative thoughts and fear were preparing ground for her spiritual disaster in the campus. She needed to realise this fear and rebuke it in Jesus name.

As children of God we should think success, talk success, and expect success in what we are embarking on, not backsliding. Yes, there will be times of tests and temptations, ups and downs, but our pre-composition of expecting the best will help us manifest the right attitude to overcome.

If an enemy wants to run you down and out he simply does things to make you afraid of him first. With that fear now operating in you, that enemy can now carry out his wish successfully.

So look deeply. What are you afraid of? It's time to deal with them.

Chapter 3: The Secret Behind the Power of Goliath and Jezebel.

Goliath and Jezebel wrought so much evil during their time. They were no doubt involved with the highest level of occultism of their time. These two individuals could symbolically pass for the devil himself. But just how did they go about wielding their power and subduing their enemies?

Goliath, an occult authority knew how to wield fear upon his opponents through bold oral intimidations and curses. That was his key to defeating his opponents.

*"Goliath stood and shouted to the ranks of Israel, "Why do you come out and line up for battle? Am I not a Philistine, and are you not the **servants of***

***Saul**? Choose a man and have him come down to me* - 1 Samuel 17:8

"Servants of Saul? "

Is that who the Israelites were?

Of course not. But Goliath made them believe that. He made them forget they were servants of the MOST HIGH God. He talked them into forgetting that God who cannot be seen has helped them defeat bigger giants in the past. He made them to look at themselves as ordinary servants of Saul.

And it worked. For as long as the Israelites saw themselves as too small to confront him, he was in charge.

The devil will do everything he can to make you think that you are a nobody; that you can't do anything; that you are just a small broom that will just get broken.

He will try to make you forget about God and what He has done for you in the past. He will inspire people who will tell you, "sister help yourself. That problem has killed so, so and so person. That spiritualist can help you." Or "brother, that woman (your wife) is evil ..... She cannot bear you a child... leave that prayer thing and be wise."

Or "hey bro, you're going down. Do you really think that by praying you can make any changes? Please face reality. Prayer simply makes you feel good, it doesn't change anything."

But these are all lies.

Goliath went on to intimidate the children of Israel. The Bible continues:

And the Philistine said, I defy the armies of Israel this day; give me a man, that we may fight together.

When Saul and all Israel **HEARD THOSE WORDS** *of the Philistine, they were dismayed, and greatly afraid -* **1 Samuel 17:10-11**

Wow! He talked them into fear of his power. That way, he defeated them even before any strike.

And all the men of Israel, when they saw the man, fled from him, and were sore afraid. - **1 Samuel 17:10-11**

The giant is not always as strong as he is claiming to be. His claims are only meant to make you submit that he is strong. Once you do, you've lost. ***The greatest power of your enemy is your fear of what he can do!***

IDENTIFY YOUR GOLIATHS

Your Goliaths are those voices shouting to you that you are doomed, that you will fail, that you won't succeed, that you will die in that illness, etc.

Anything that is trying to show you how small you are is your Goliath.

When you notice some symptoms in your body and maybe diagnosed (let's say) of arthritis, how do you react? Your mind will whisper to you at least hundred reasons why you should be scared and start running to and fro. People will tell you how many persons have died through that disease. Many things will also happen to convince you, it's a terrible, killer disease.

However, all those voices are intended by the devil to get you afraid. Once you become afraid, you've submitted, you've given up. You'll subsequently remain the slave of the disease, which will now make your body a playground.

Any message, information or news that tries to increase your fear is your Goliath that must be killed with everything you've got. No sickness or disease is too strong that you cannot be healed. That many people have prayed for you here and there without you getting healed, does not mean you will no longer be healed. That an expert has confirmed your case impossible does not mean you will go down by it. That it has killed this and that person does not mean it will kill you.

Don't let the hidden voices of the devil and your mind state otherwise. That was what Goliath did to the Israelites. He told them how powerful he was and how many people he's killed and how little they can do. Through that the Israelites became afraid. He became their master.

Dr Uma Ukpai said, "we do not measure our enemies by the size of their guns, but the size of their gods."

Locate your Goliaths today and confront them. Those inner voices of fear and defeat, rise and shout at them to keep quiet. Tell them that you are going forward and that nothing will stop you.

THEY HAD TO MAKE THEM AFRAID IF THEY MUST CAPTURE THEM.

The enemies of God's people always know that without making them afraid, they cannot capture them.

> *"Then they called out in Hebrew to the people of Jerusalem who were on the wall, to terrify them and make them afraid in order to capture the city."*
>
> **- 2 Chronicles 32:18**

Just look at that! They can only capture them if they have made them afraid.

Wow!

What does that tell you?

Your enemy will first and foremost do things to make you afraid. It is when you now have some of those fears that he finally captures you in that very area you got afraid. Beware!

We too can equally bring any problem or storm down to our feet if we learn to boldly talk them to fear, confrontationally, authoritatively and violently. For instance, the moment you start telling that sickness in your body, *"you are a stranger"*... *"You are not permitted to stay in my body"* ... *"my body is the temple of the Holy Spirit"* .... *"Just as Jesus cursed the fig tree and it withered from the roots, I curse you to wither out of my body"*

The moment you begin to speak authoritatively in this manner every day, irrespective of the pain, sooner than you expect, that sickness will leave. It might seem to persist for some time, but it will soon get afraid by your threats and take off.

HOW DO PEOPLE RESPOND TO THREATS FROM SUPER POWERS?

You see, the same way people get *"**fear-full**"* when they are threatened by some high-power fellows is the way your problems get fearful –when you threaten them with your words. You know why? Because you are the master of your life.

Also notice that those who threaten others don't close their mouths to do it. They speak. They say things that put fear on their targets' minds. That is the way problems, diseases and storms of life respond, too.

When God says he will put fear and terror on your enemies, it means that as you open your mouth every day and continually speak threatening scriptures against those problems and mountains that confront you, fear will eventually come on them and soon, they'll take off. God will not put your enemies to fear if you don't speak scriptural threatening words against them.

ENTER JEZEBEL

Jezebel was another evil figure in the Bible. She was a witch who mastered the art of using fear to overrun her enemies. Once this fear is in them she automatically subdues them to her will.

She once used that trick on Elijah, and Elijah, though a mighty man of God nearly got drowned – until he waited on the LORD. It dawned on him that he was actually greater than what he was running from. With that anger he went back to Jezebel and cursed her. And she died. (1 king 19, 21:20-24).

It seems to me that fear is something we have to

regularly guard against. No matter our depth in God, the spiritual Jezebels and Goliaths never give up. They will create events and circumstances intended to kindle fear in us and subsequently chase us out of God's plans for our lives.

Just like Elijah did, when we seem to be overwhelmed with fear, worry and depression, waiting on the LORD in fasting and prayer will revive our spirits and give us the boldness to confront whatever it is we are afraid of.

Always remember that you are greater than whatever you are faced with. The burden is always equal to the horse's strength. Just like Elijah, receive strength from God and speak to your fears and threats.

Chapter 4: **Fruits of Fear and Worry.**

1. FEAR HINDERS OR DELAYS GOD'S INTERVENTION IN A PERSON'S LIFE DURING A TIME OF CRITICAL NEED

Fearful actions during times of seeming danger are more dangerous than the seeming danger itself. In ministering to the sick and demon oppressed, it is often better to first and foremost attack the spirit of fear and let the person realize how he must cooperate with the minister by shunning all voices of doubt and fear in his mind. When this is taken care of properly, the deliverance often manifests quicker than we expect. If not, there is usually an irritating delay.

Even if the person receives deliverance because of

the anointing and faith of the minister, if the receiver is not schooled as fast as possible on how to resist fear with God's Words daily, he is likely to fall victim to the same problems again...sometimes, even deeper than he was before deliverance attempts.

An older minister friend of mine, Dr. Ben Okoro, who has now gone to be with the LORD, learned this lesson in a very exceptional way. Years before he went to be with the LORD, he was spiritually attacked and was bedridden for two years plus. Several times he would go into a coma and then come back again. In fact, the best word to use is half-dead, for he died many times and came back to life. I interviewed him and compiled his testimony in a book after his recovery. While talking with him he confessed that he later knew where his major problem lied. He said, "I believe that my major problem was fear. I saw myself overwhelmed with the highest degree of fear; that became a ground for the enemy to do all the things he did in my life."

He learned that the thousands of prayers offered on his behalf by many saints were delayed because he believed his fears. He believed that God was done with him and that he was going to die. It was when he started to doubt the things he was afraid of that his deliverance began to take place.

In his book, Walking in the Miraculous, Bishop David Oyedepo shared a testimony about a brother who was travelling by sea with some other fellows. On the way they were hit by a furious storm that destroyed their boat. They all fell into the water, but this brother, while falling, courageously shouted,

"Jesus, I refuse to die!"

According to the testimony, something that looked like a stick came close to him and he held it. As a result, he stayed floating. When a rescue team eventually arrived after three days of search he was rescued.

The most incredible part of the story is that when he was rescued, he looked to see what it was he was holding onto, that had kept him afloat, but found nothing. It was certainly the name of Jesus.

Every act of faith always invites God into a situation, while every act of fear invites Satan. Fear always hinders and delays God's intervention even when a serious danger is threatening.

Pray to the *LORD to keep your faith on fire every day.*

2. FEAR MAKES A PERSON UNPRODUCTIVE

In Matthew chapter 25: 14-30, Jesus told a now famous story of the talents. One of the men refused to invest his money. When propped for the reason he didn't trade with the money, he said:

... *"I was afraid, and went and hid thy talent in the earth"*

If he had invested and lost the money, it would have been a different ball game. His master would not have given him the harshest punishment. But for not making any attempts out of fear, his master instructed to *"...cast the unprofitable servant into outer darkness where there shall be weeping and gnashing of teeth"* (vs 30).

I came across an interesting piece of advice some time ago that said, ***"If you think investing is too risky, then wait until you are handed the bill for not investing."***

Life is full of risks. If you try to avoid the risks, you'll live a very small life. The Bible says:

"Cast your bread upon the waters for after many days you will find it again. Give portion to seven, yes to eight, for you do not know what disaster may come upon the land.

"Whoever watches the wind will not plant; whoever looks at the could will not reap.

Sow your seed in the morning and at evening let not your hand be idle, for you do not know which will succeed, whether this or that, or whether both will do equally well - **Ecclesiastes 11:1-6**

That's talking about investing in multiple businesses. Not because all will succeed, but at least some will.

It's okay to do a proper analysis before you put money in any venture, but's it's equally terrible to over analyse. The problem with over analysis is that you see more reasons why it can't be done than reasons why it can be done.

When the analysis becomes too much, make sure you are not guided by fear. Listen to your inner man and explore.

---

3. FEAR TORMENTS

Fear has torturing effects. It can be a gateway to spiritual attacks, evil dreams, nightmares and all kinds of torments in one's life. The bible says:

"There is no fear in love; but perfect love casteth out fear: because fear hath torment. He that feareth is not made perfect in love." - **1 John 4:18**

Fear is a spirit that chokes the love of God from full manifestation. Whenever fear attempts to raise its ugly head in your life, cut it off with the SWORD of the Spirit.

4. FEAR BRINGS UNBELIEF

All acts of unbelief and doubt stem from fear, and you remember that unbelief is sin. "A **doubt-full** and **unbelief –full**" person, the bible says cannot please God (James 1:5-8).

The ten spies were afraid of the giants, the descendants of Arak, because of their size. Their fear led them to doubt the power of God. They convinced others to follow their fear. Unfortunately, the result was terrible. They did not enter the Promised Land.

Permitting the size of your obstacles and problems to make you afraid is very dangerous. The moment you begin to look at your size and the size of the situation before you and become afraid, you will grow doubts and unbelief and when these are in you, you block God from coming to your rescue.

---

5. FEAR ENDANGERS ONE TO ETERNAL PUNISHMENT

Revelation 21:8 says:

"But the fearful, and unbelieving and the abominable and murderers, and whoremongers, and sorcerers, and idolaters, and all liars, shall have their part in the lake which burneth with fire

and brimstone, which is the second death."

Notice that the *'fear-full'* and the **unbelieving** are classified with murderers, idolaters, sorcerers, liars, the abominable and the other sinners. "That's a pretty ugly crowd" you don't want to belong to.

Fear is actually much more serious than we think. That's because fear takes us out of faith, making us do things that do not please God.

*"And **without faith it is impossible to please God**, because anyone who comes to him must believe that he exists and that he rewards those who earnestly seek him"* – **Hebrews 11:6**.

Chapter 5: Eleven Types of Fear to Deal With.

There are about ten forms of fears we must get rid out of our lives.

1. THE FEAR OF SIN

Some people have told me, *"The only thing I fear is sin"*. They say this with a sense that looks like that of one whose aim is to live holy and please God, without knowing that they are victims of ignorance.

You and I are not to be afraid of sin. We are rather asked to take decision against it. The simple knowledge that any form of sinful act is a step to disgrace according to proverb 14:34 is enough to get you to say, *"I am taking a decision today against sin. God help me by your spirit to walk on the path of righteousness every day".*

Your decision against sin is better than being always afraid of falling into sin. If you are always afraid of falling into sin, you can't escape your fears. What you fear you attract. But what we decide against, we avoid.

> *"For whatsoever is born of God overcometh the world: and this is the victory that overcometh the world – even our faith. We know that whosoever is born of God sinneth not; but he that is begotten of God keepeth himself, and that wicked one toucheth him not."* – **1 John 5:14-18.**

Every Christian has an inbuilt *Strong Machine* that fights to resist sin every day. What we simply need to do is recognize this in-built *Strong Machine* and cooperate with **Him**. When opportunities to sin present themselves, this **Sin-Resistant Machine** in us usually starts blowing an alarm. He starts getting us uncomfortable about the plan. Cooperating with **Him** at such times is the key to victory over sin.

We should be able to distinguish between what it means to desire to please God always and what it means to be afraid of falling into sin. Job was always afraid he might fall into sin and as a result lost his riches. That fear didn't help him.

PRAYER

"I am greater than sin. I am made in God's image. I am above sin. The seed of God is in me. So I cannot sin. The power of sin has been broken in my life.

*Lord, quicken the **Sin-Resistance Engine** in me every day and lead me by Your Spirit to cooperate* *in the mighty name of Jesus.*

---

2. THE FEAR OF DANGER.

This is a simple experiment. Board a commercial vehicle to some far city and study the emotional structure of the passengers with you. When any little thing shakes the bus you see almost everyone whining in fear. They do not know that such negative obsession of a possible disaster has the power to create such realities.

> *"Thou shalt not be afraid for the terror by night; nor for the arrow that flieth by day." -* **Psalms 91:5**

Undeniably, these things characterize our world and immediate environment. But those who trust God have no cause to fear. They will come and go, but the child of God will remain unhurt. However, the child of God who finds himself nurture fears for such things and does nothing serious to send those fears away as soon as possible may find himself a victim of such evils sooner or later.

When a person's mind is filled with thoughts, imaginations and fears of some kind of danger, that person is not too far from it.

I have listed a couple of scriptures below, where God speaks strongly of protecting us continually. Should one want to embark on a journey or suddenly begin to develop some fears of danger, it's just a matter of taking your Bible, locating those verses, reading them as many times as possible to yourself until you believe them; and then pray with them. After taking these steps one should be about his business because God cannot break his word. His word is his power.

But if a person suddenly begins to develop some fears of danger and does nothing about it, as I said before, that person is close to it!

Please note that the fear of danger is quite different from a spiritual discernment of a coming danger. The Bible tells us that the Holy Spirit will give us knowledge of certain things beforehand so we can be prepared to receive them (if they are good ones) or avert them (if they are bad ones). Someone may get these revelations sometimes. They may come through a dream, word of knowledge, prophecy or inner conviction. When a person gets this kind of discernment what he should do is simply search the scriptures and locate God's words against such demonic plans, and with them pray. After which he should go about his business and never be afraid of those evils.

In our church sometimes, we do receive some revelation or dream or prophecy about a possible attack to come from the enemy, in the form of armed robbers, accidents, spiritual attacks, etc. When we receive such revelations what we do is set apart one day or two for fasting and authoritative prayers against such plans. When we are done, we go about our business fearing nothing. The devil has lost.

That you or someone else had a dream or prophecy or whatever about a possible attack from the enemy coming against you should not make you scared.

Thank God for it and pick the Bible, locate what god has said about your continual protection and deliverance from danger, and use those promises to cancel such plans. When you are done, simply go about your business, fearing nothing anymore, and always remind yourself of what God says.

Even though I walk through the valley of the shadow of death I will fear no evil **-Psalm 23:4**

A thousand shall fall at thy side and ten thousand at the right hand; but it shall not come nigh thee; only with thine eyes shall thou behold and see the reward of the wicked. - **Psalm 91:7-8**.

---

3. FEAR OF DEATH

Death is not just for a force – it is a spirit person that moves, talks an acts. Fear is the greatest weapon that this spirit has. When someone allows the ***fear of dying*** to consume him, he is likely to die quicker.

One Of The Reason For Christ Is shameful Death On The Cross Is To Deliver Those Who Believe In Him From the fear of death.

Hebrew chapter 11 tells us how the early followers of Christ were not afraid of dying; even when threatened with death, it didn't matter to them because they knew that death's power is it's fear. They understood that even if they died, it would be a transition to a better life.

Jesus said:

"I am he that liveth, and was dead; and, behold, I am alive for evermore, Amen; and have the keys of hell and of death." - **Revelation 1:18**

The Keys Of Death Here Talks About The Power Which Death Has –Which 'he' Uses To Kill People. Jesus Now Holds It.

Imagine that someone is pointing a pistol on another person and threatening to pull the trigger. Get this straight! This fellow's power is the gun in his hand, nothing else. Without that gun, he is flat and could be beaten blue black by the guy he is threatening.

Then imagine that a smarter guy overrun's this fellow and takes out the gun from him, what happens next?

I assure you, the hard guy's power and boasting and vile is over. He might end up a meat in vulture's den that day.

That is exactly what Jesus did to death. He collected

the ***power of death***, and till eternity he is still holding it.

So why should you be afraid of death?

You give death power to kill – you submit to him to deal with you with his mere hands - when you nurture his fear in you, or allow it in your mind.

Apostle Paul Understood These Mysteries so Much That He Dribbled Death The Way He Wanted. When He Was Threatened, He Said:

For to me, to live is Christ and to die is gain. If I am to go on living in the body, this will mean fruitful labor for me. Yet what shall I choose? I do not know!

I am torn between the two: I desire to depart and be with Christ, which is better by far; but it is more necessary for you that I remain in the body. Convinced of this, I know that I will remain, and I will continue with all of you for your progress and joy in the faith, - **Philippians 1:21-25 (NIV)**

That's like playing on the intelligence of Mr Death. He could choose whether to continue here on earth or to go over there in heaven. Eventually, he choose to remain.

Beloved, God has promised that you will fulfil your days. You will not die before your time. When Mr Death comes threatening tell 'him' to shut up and don't move until he does. He doesn't have that former power he had before the death of Christ. 'His' threats now are to convince you to fear him and when you do, you lose. The Bible says:

"Since the children have flesh and blood, he too

shared in their humanity so that by his death he might break the power of him who holds the power of death—that is, the devil—and free those who all their lives were held in slavery by their fear of death. - **Hebrews 2:14-15 (NIV).**

The fear of death will make you a slave to the forces of darkness. When you allow your mind to be occupied with death, death, death, God cannot help it. Unless you react fast against this mind game, various circumstances will work out your thoughts and fears.

That you or someone else dreamt and saw you or a member of your family dead is not a sign that you or that loved one will die. Rather, a sign that you (or that loved one) will live. To accommodate any fear because of such a dream is giving the devil power to birth the dream faster. What you should do in such a situation is to thank God, and search the scriptures yourself. Locate God's promises for your long life and then cancel the plan; after which you can go about your business.

---

4. THE FEAR OF CRITICISM OR WHAT PEOPLE WILL SAY.

The fear of criticism paralyses vision, kills enthusiasm, leads to procrastination and compromise. The fear of what people will say kills ones creative ability and makes a person docile and live by public opinion. ***The fear of what they will say is very dangerous. It is an enemy of action.***

Peter once gave in to this kind of fear. The result?

He unconsciously began to compromise his very stand on salvation (see Galatians 2:11-13). The fear of criticism – what they will say - is one of the greatest obstacles to a fulfilled life.

Unless you completely close your ears to **what they will say**– or what they are already saying - you won't hear more of what God is saying. As a matter of fact, your fear of **what they will say** will not stop them from talking anyway. So what's the use?

Be poor, they will talk. Be rich, they will talk. Be sick, they will talk. Be healthy, they will talk. Try hard in life, they will talk. Be lazy, they will talk.

What will you do or want to do in your life that people will not talk?

Nothing!

People will always talk. If you do well, they will talk. If you miss it, they will talk.

I Read About A Man Who Committed Suicide Because Whatever He Did, People Misunderstood Him And Talk Against It. So, He got tired of criticism and killed himself.

Very Sad.

Unfortunately, People Still Criticised Him Harshly for what he did.

I believe that until the world ends, people will not stop finding faults and talking. In fact, I have concluded that **critics and faultfinders are just unpaid advertisers. They should not be treated as enemies. They are very useful in giving a man FREE publicity.**

Whenever God starts taking a man to a higher level in life, the first way you notice it is how people start talking against that person here and there. It's amazing, but it's just so. You can't stop it.

People must talk against what they cannot do. Those who talk against others are always behind those they talk against. And the best way to reply a critic or criticism is to have an outstanding record of success. Time will always force wisdom out.

---

5. THE FEAR OF WHAT MEN WILL DO.

How often do you change your plans or refrain from telling the truth because you are afraid of a particular person in your office or field? The fear of what a person will do to you will always make you look 'inferior' and unable to protest for your right. It will make you an "O yes member". It can even steal the fear of God from you and make you die in silence.

We should never measure a person by his size, statements or boasting; measure him by the size of his god – not even by "the size of his gun", or cash.

If a person threatens you and you become afraid and change your plans or compromise your faith, then you don't know your God. Remember Shedrach, Meshack and Abednego? The size and army of Nebuchadnezzar did not make them shift their ground. Why? Because they knew their God.

Stand for the truth. No man has power over your life. They may threaten, they may boast. But they cannot bring you down eventually. Jesus said:

"Are not too sparrows sold for a penny? Yet not one

of them will fall to the ground apart from the will of your Father…..and even the very hairs of your head are all numbered. So don't be afraid; you are worth more than many sparrows. - Matthew 10:29-31

"The lord is my light and my salvation – whom shall I fear? The lord is the strong hold of my life – of whom shall I be afraid?

"When evil men advance against me to devour my flesh, when my enemies and my foes attack, they stumble and fall. Though an army besiege me, my heart will not fear; though war break out against me, even then will I be confident.– Psalm 27:1-3.

Do Not Be Afraid Of Them, For I Am With You, And Will Rescue You…- Jeremiah **1:8.**

As you read this scriptures you may say, "Well, I got

that, no problem". But that is not enough. They actually mean what they say. Convince yourself about those promises.

We are not saying that bad fellows will not in any way want to advance against you. They will. But you must never allow any fear in your mind. Just keep reminding yourself about those promises. With them take authority and arrest the situation spiritually. As you keep reminding yourself of these WORDS, they will eventually succumb.

Suppose someone confronts you one day say, "You will see." How do you respond? There is no need for you to start shaking, looking for someone to pray over you. Stand there and boldly reply that person, "You too will see. God will fight you".

What is your confidence? God says he will fight

against those who fight against you and rescue you. So that settles it.

But when you begin to shiver and run up and down, you grant Satan the power to fulfil what that fellow said and wish.

As a child of God, you are not just an ordinary person. God forbid. You are God's image and representative wherever you find yourself. Whatever can't harm God, is not supposed to harm you.

If someone claims before you that he is a "witch or occult man" and promises you hell and thunder. Don't go to your house and begin to cry. Stand there and reply him that you have the greatest "power man" behind you. Tell him that Jesus is the man. And that because he has said such a thing he too will see Jesus in battle. That is how to put Christ to action. And that was exactly what David did and killed Goliath.

> "The Fear of man bringeth a snare: But whoso putted his trust in the Lord shall be safe. – Proverbs 29:25.

---

6. THE FEAR OF POVERTY OR FAILURE IN BUSINESS

If you are always afraid that you might be poor or fail in a particular venture or endeavour, the probability that you will not make it is certain. Riches, poverty or failure are created first in the mind before they manifest physically. As a man thinketh in his heart, so is he.

> *If they obey and serve him, they shall spend their days in prosperity, and their years in pleasures. –*

Job 36:11.

God is saying that you have no reason to be scared of poverty. He is assuring you that you'll spend your days in abundance. So when an iota of fear begins to crop up in your mind regarding how the daily needs will be met, run to God's WORD and comfort yourself.

Can any one of you by worrying add a single hour to your life? "And why do you worry about clothes? See how the flowers of the field grow. They do not labor or spin. Yet I tell you that not even Solomon in all his splendor was dressed like one of these. If that is how God clothes the grass of the field, which is here today and tomorrow is thrown into the fire, will he not much more clothe you--you of little faith? – Matthew 6:27-29

7. THE FEAR OF ILLNESS.

Are you always nurturing fears of contracting any sickness sooner or later? Is the fear of being barren or unable to produce children occasionally found in you? Do you get worried because many people have prayed for you over an illness, yet no physical sign of healing? Are you concerned or thinking that you may no longer get healed?

Now is the time to cast out these fears.

That many people have prayed for you without you getting healed does not mean you will no longer be healed – or that it is now God's will for you to remain sick. Not at all. God still wants to heal you. So keep demanding your healing.

Experts have reported that 75% of sick patients do not get healed because of fear and anxiety over their situations. They say that when a person is afraid that he might not recover from any illness, that their drugs can do little or nothing to assist.

The Fear of any situation is always more serious than the situation.

Arise and speak to your fear of ill health now to cease in the name of Jesus Christ. God will continue to protect you from the diseases and illnesses that fly around. And if you are sick in any part of your body, you will be healed. It's not over with you.

"Bless the LORD, O my soul, And forget none of His benefits; 3Who pardons all your iniquities, Who heals all your diseases; 4Who redeems your life

from the pit, Who crowns you with loving kindness and compassion". - **Psalm 103:2-4**

The wife of a prominent man of God fell sick and was told by the experts that she had only few days to live – based on their diagnosis and analysis. Her husband, a powerful preacher, prayed and prayed and invited other men of God to pray, yet nothing happened. Her case continued to worsen. With just few days to the experts' date remaining, this woman mustered some strength, settled down and located forty scriptures on God's health and healing plan. As she continued to read, meditate on and minister to herself with those scriptures, the sickness (whatever they called it) eventually disappeared. And she returned to her business.

You see, the word of God is not just a literature. It

carries life. If you are having any attack of illness in your body, rather than worry and fear, locate God's Words about your health and stay with them for some time. These days, there are literatures that make it easier to locate these promises of healing and use them for personal prayers and ministration.

Staying with the WORD to meditate over and pray with in any situation you find yourself is the quickest and surest way to overcome any fear, worry and adverse situation.

---

8. THE FEAR OF DEMONS AND SPIRITS.

Some time ago, a friend of mine invited me to pray for a woman. When we go to the sister's house, she narrated her case and it was quite pathetic. But while praying, the LORD ministered to me that this woman's real problem was the fear of demons and their power. I paused and confronted her with what the LORD put in my spirit and encouraged her to let go the fear of witches and the powers of darkness. I showed her some verses of the Bible to always read, memorise, pray with and stand on.

A couple of days later, my friend told me I had actually hit that woman's main problem. He told me that this sister had being so bound by the spirit of fear that if an ordinary lizard passes by her suddenly she would start crying and shouting that they have come again. She would start binding demons and casting evil spirits. She would hear a noise in the midnight and wake up and begin to cry to God to deliver her from her enemies.

Being afraid of witches, demons, occult power, what

they can and will do is very destructive. The only thing a child of God should do when he senses a demonic attack against his life is to stand strong on what the bible says and return fire.

You, little children, are from God and have overcome them, because greater is He who is in you than he who is in the world. – 1 John 4:4

They overcome him (the devil) by the blood of the lamb and by the word of their testimony. – Revelation 12:11

The BIBLE did not say we "will" overcome, making it a future tense. It says we have already overcome.

I have always maintained that the problem is not the spiritual attacks one claims he or she is having, the main problem is ignorance. For instance, apply the above scriptures to your situation; you will see that you have already overcome the attack through the BLOOD of Jesus.

If a demonic attack in your life and family looks serious, then be more serious with The Word of Your Testimony – the WORD of God - and Let's See who will stand.

Our closed mouths, on many occasions, are the major reason behind the beating and persistence demonic attacks we keep having. When we start using scriptures to reject those demonic attacks, oppressions and manipulations, we'll see things start changing.

> *"I will give you the keys of the kingdom of heaven; whatever you bind on earth will be[a] bound in heaven, and whatever you loose on earth will be[b] loosed in heaven."* - Matthew 16:19 (NIV).

"Truly I tell you, whatever you bind on earth will be[a] bound in heaven, and whatever you loose on earth will be[b] loosed in heaven. - **Matthew 18:18(NIV)**

Whenever you sense any form of attack on your life, use these scriptures to take authority over the demons and command them to get into abyss.

---

9. THE FEAR OF POSSIBLE DISAPPOINTMENT IN MARRIAGE.

95% of this fear is mostly found in women. That means that women fear more of not being loved or being disappointed in their marriage. Some men nurse this fear equally, but it is more noticeable in women.

Napoleon Hill, in his book, Think and Grow Rich,

said, "our brains become magnetised with the dominating thoughts which hold in our mind and, by means which no man is familiar, these magnets attract to us the forces, the people , the circumstance of life which harmonise with the nature of our dominating thought"

That's just affirming the Bible statement that "as a man thinketh in his heart, so is he" (Proverbs 23:7). If a person continues to harbour fear of losing love, he or she will unsuspectingly start doing things that will eventually make that fear become a reality.

For example, whenever a person starts developing unnecessary suspicion of his spouse or friend without reasonable evidence of sufficient grounds – this fear is at work. When person starts incurring more than is within his pocket in order to please his spouse —this fear is at work. When a person finds himself remembering his spouse past faults at the slightest provocation — this fear is at work.

There may be other signals not stated. The point is if you start noticing any kind of fear of losing love or fear of getting divorced or getting thrown out of your home, you need to quickly realize what's happening in your mind and arrest the situation.

---

10 THE FEAR OF THE FUTURE.

"No One Knows Tomorrow!"

Right?

Sure.

But whatever comes up tomorrow, we know it's going to be to our favour. How do we know?

Because we're following the ONE who knows tomorrow…THE LORD JESUS. So we can quickly relax, knowing that He is there for us.

Tomorrow holds great things for you. Your ministry will grow larger. It will not fail in any way. More people will get blessed through your works.

Your marriage will continue getting better and better. You will not die. Your children will continue to grow from strength to strength. You will not contract any illness.

That should be your belief about your tomorrow.

God Says:

> "I know the plan I have for you. Plans to prosper you and not harm you, plans to give you hope a future." - Jeremiah 29:11

"No Eye Has Seen, No Ear Has Heard, No Mind Has Conceived What God Has Prepared For Those Who Love Him." - 1 Corinthians 2:7.

That's why you should not be afraid of tomorrow and what it holds. *"What the righteous desire will be Granted"* (Proverbs 10:24)

God is faithful to His WORDS.

"The LORD is my shepherd; I shall not be in want." - Psalm 23:1

"The lions may grow weak and hungry, but those who seek the LORD lack no good thing." - Psalm 34:10

"I was young and now and I am old and yet I have never seen the righteous forsaken or their children begging bread." - Psalm 37:25

Those are reasons not to be afraid of tomorrow and what the future holds.

---

11. THE FEAR OF OLD AGE.

Good News. "Better is the end of a thing than the beginning thereof." (Ecclesiastes 7:8).

Caleb said:

"I am today 85 years old, I am still as strong as today as the day when Moses sent me out, and I am just as vigorous to go out to battle now as I was then" - Joshua 14:10-11

Caleb's God is our God. He is the same yesterday, today and forever. So there is no fear of growing old. There is grace to be strong, healthy, sound and ever flourishing.

"The righteous will flourish like a palm tree, they will grow in the house of the LORD, they will flourish in the courts of our God, they will bear fruit even in old age, and they will stay fresh and green - Psalm 92:12-14.

Hallelujah. God's WORD is YEA and Amen. So in old age you will still be strong and bear fruit.

SUMMARY.

Above are the eleven faces of the dragons...FEAR, WORRRY and DEPRESSION. These are ten areas we can unsuspectingly nurture fear. But God's WORDS has given us victory in those areas. So we can approach these aspects of life with boldness knowing that He who has promised is faithful and will accomplish that which He promised.

Chapter 6: How to Defeat Fear, Worry and Depression Permanently.

What are the things you fear, worry and get depressed about?

It's time to address these fears right now. It's time to bind and cast these demons out and claim your peace and joy.

1. DISCOVER WHAT YOU REALLY FEAR, WORRY OR GET DEPRESSED ABOUT.

Let's do some work. It's possible that what gets you afraid in life or bother your peace of mind is in the eleven faces of the dragon that I have listed in chapter 5. Let's look deep and identify the real issues we fear and worry about.

Is your major fears or worry about:

- Sin

- Danger

- Death

- Criticisms or what people will say or are already saying.

- Poverty and failure in business

- Illness

- Demons and their attacks and nightmares.

- Loss of love or marriage failure.

- The future

- Old age

Yea, these are not the only things people fear or worry about in life, which also brings them depression. Those are just summaries that God has laid in my heart.

The point however is to identify these things that cause us fear, worry and depression. Take a plain piece of paper and list the things that seem to border and get you really scared. Once we can pin point these issues, we can now deal with them appropriately.

2. EXPLORE DAVID'S STRATEGY.

There was a time in David's life that circumstances and negative events pressed him hard enough to develop fears all round. What did he do? How did he handle such times in his life?

He said:

> *"I sought the LORD and He delivered me from all my fears"* – Psalm 34:4

He Sought God in prayers and He delivered him from "all his fears!" Not One. Not Two, Not Three. They must have been so many.

It's possible that we suddenly begin to have fears in our hearts due to the way things are going in the home, office or the nation. It's really possible that our fears are justifiable. But the truth is that these fears do not produce good fruits eventually.

Whenever you notice you are developing fears all around, probably because of unusual disappointments, frustrations, delayed answers to prayers, etc., your next best action should be to declare a season of rest in God's presence until your confidence and faith is completely restored. This rest could be a season of fasting and prayers or personal retreat to read the Bible and meditate.

It's important that you don't get carried away with being busy, ignore your fears and live like all is well. Don't. Take some time out and deal with your fears and let God restore your confidence and direction.

"Call to me and I will answer you and tell you great and unsearchable things you do not know."–

Jeremiah 33:3

---

3. LEARN TO START REJECTING FEAR "PASSING WORDS"

Words are spiritual forces that create physical

realities. Just as the Israelites bought their fear and defeat through the words they heard from Goliath, we can also let fear into our hearts by the words we hear. These words may be the news we watch, what the doctors are saying, what neighbours think and say about us, what teachers say about our children, etc.

To continue to manifest victory over fear, worry and depression, we must learn how to reject news and words that build up our fears. Just as faith comes from WORDS (of GOD), fear also comes through WORDS (Romans 10:17).

Jesus has already told us that in the world there will be a lot of tribulations, but that we have peace in Him. Prophet Isaiah too said that gross darkness will cover the earth and the peoples, but that our light will shine (Isaiah 60:1-3). So when men come up with their analyses on how terrible things are going to become, we should fine rest in God's WORDS and reject all this evil news everywhere.

---

4. SPEAK TO YOURSELF

There's no one who doesn't come to a point in time when fear and worry is justifiable. However, how we handle such moments matter a lot. When you're faced with situations that raise fear, worry and depression, spend time to speak to yourself morning and night. As you steadfastly talk to yourself with God's words, these fears and worries will leave and you'll have the energy to face what's happening and receive grace to overcome.

For example, if the rent and other bills are due and

there is no money to pay, you're justifiably going to have some fears and worries. But as you continue to speak to yourself, you can replace your fears with faith, confidence and divine support.

I Keep Telling Myself,

"Daniel, don't worry, you will make it. God is with you. He cannot disappoint you. He is seriously at work in all these situations. Be rest assured that everything is working out for your own good. So don't be afraid. Relax."

As I keep talking and speaking to myself in that manner, quoting scriptures as well, the Holy Spirit takes over and reassures my spirit that all will be well. I can then smile and laugh even in the midst of what's happening.

5. PRAYING IN TONGUES

We may not be able to delve into the subject of praying in tongues in this book. It's got to be a separate book entirely. This is because we won't do the subject justice here. However, if you're baptized with the Holy Spirit with the evidence of speaking in tongues, when you're faced with fears and worries and depression, ask the Holy Spirit for grace and pray in tongues for long. Your fears and worries will give way and you'll receive spiritual edification and restoration. those who are baptised with the Holy Spirit When we pray in tongues, we edify ourselves.

Be filled with the Spirit – **Ephesians 5:18**

I would like every one of you to speak in tongues…I thank God that I speak in tongues more than all of you. Therefore, my brothers, be eager to prophesy, and do not forbid speaking in tongues. – **1 Corinthians 14:5, 18, 39.**

Build Yourselves in Your Most Holy Faith and Pray in The Holy Spirit. - **Jude 20.**

Chapter 7: Prayers to Cast Out Fear, Worry, Depression and Panic Attacks.

Are you overwhelmed with fear and worries? Are you feeling depressed? Are you suffering from panic attacks? The prayers below will give you deliverance and restore your energy, confidence and faith for living. So please pray these prayers with all your heart and trust God for answers.

GOD'S PROMISES.

1. 2 Timothy 1:7 - *For God hath not given us the spirit of fear; but of power, and of love, and of a sound mind.*

2. Isaiah 41:10 - *Fear thou not; for I am with thee: be not dismayed; for I am thy God: I will* *strengthen thee; yea, I will help thee; yea, I will uphold thee with the right hand of my righteousness.*

---

3. 1 John 4:18 - *There is no fear in love; but perfect love casteth out fear: because fear hath torment. He that feareth is not made perfect in love.*

---

4. Psalms 34:4 - *I sought the LORD, and he heard me, and delivered me from all my fears.*

---

5. Philippians 4:6 - *Be careful for nothing; but in every thing by prayer and supplication with thanksgiving let your requests be made known unto God.*

6. Romans 8:15 - *For ye have not received the spirit of bondage again to fear; but ye have received the Spirit of adoption, whereby we cry, Abba, Father.*

7. Psalms 56:3-4 - *What time I am afraid, I will trust in thee. In God I will praise his word, in God I have put my trust; I will not fear what flesh can do unto me.*

8. Isaiah 43:1-3 - *But now thus saith the LORD that created thee, O Jacob, and he that formed thee, O Israel, Fear not: for I have redeemed thee, I have called [thee] by thy name; thou [art] mine*

9. Deuteronomy 7:21 - *Thou shalt not be afraid at them: for the LORD thy God [is] among you, a mighty God and terrible.*

---

10. Joshua 1:9 - *Have not I commanded thee? Be strong and of a good courage; be not afraid, neither be thou dismayed: for the LORD thy God [is] with thee whithersoever thou goest.*

PRAYER OF SURRENDER.

"Dear LORD Jesus Christ,

"I know that all power and authority on Heaven and Earth belongs to You alone.

"I come to You today, asking for deliverance from fear, worries, depression and panic attacks.

"I am facing numerous issues that are frightening me, sometimes upsetting me!

"LORD Jesus, I ask You right in faith and with all of my existence, please deliver me from all fear, worry and depression.

"Give me peace, joy and boldness to serve you all the days of my life.

"I completely surrender to YOU this day, O LORD. I surrender my spirit, soul and body to YOU.

"I know You are able to keep them safe even unto eternal life.

"Therefore LORD Jesus, I pray, take these fears, worries and hopelessness and strengthen me against them! In Jesus name.

"Protect me from every lie of the enemy that has

come my way trying to deceive me.

"I recognize that You have told me: "Let not your heart be troubled, neither let it be afraid." - John 14:27.

"Right now, I give it all to You Jesus. In Jesus name.

PROPHETIC DECLARATION.

1.

"The LORD is my light and my salvation; whom shall I fear? The LORD is the strength of my life; of whom shall I be afraid? When the wicked, even mine enemies and my foes, came upon me to eat up my flesh, they stumbled and fell. Though an host should encamp against me, my heart shall not fear: though war should rise against me, in this will I be

confident. (Psalm 27:1-3).

2.

"I announce that greater is the One that is in me than any devil on the side of my enemies.

3.

"It is written, The righteous is as bold as a lion. By my faith in Christ Jesus, I am righteous. I receive my divine boldness.

4.

"The angels of the LORD encampeth round about them that fear Him. The angels of God are with me,

I have no basis to fear any man, any evil, and any evil spirit. I have no basis to worry or be depressed.

5.

"Because the LORD of hosts is with me, I take my confidence in Him. It is written If God be for us who can be against us? God is with me, I have no enough reason to fear, worry or be depresses, in the name of Jesus.

6.

"It is written, The LORD is my light and my salvation whom shall I fear? The Lord is the defense of my life of whom shall I be afraid? Though a host of demons encamp against me, my

heart will not fear; though war rises against me, even in this I shall be confident.

7.

"The Lord is with me like a mighty terrible one. I am not afraid. I cannot be threatened. My persecutors shall stumble and fumble. Their everlasting confusion and disgrace shall never be forgotten. In Jesus name.

8.

"God has commanded me to fear not. Of the 366 days in a year, no single day is allowed for me to fear. So, I refuse to be afraid of anything. You spirit of fear, worry and depression, you are not in God's

agenda for me. I dismiss you from my life now, in the name of Jesus.

9.

"Jesus said even the very hairs of my head are not only counted but numbered. Not one single strand can be removed without God's knowledge and permission. Therefore, I put my confidence in the LORD, Who takes so such care of me. In Jesus name.

PRAYER POINTS

1.

"Father, In the name of Jesus, I refuse to fear, worry and be depressed henceforth, because God

has not given me the spirit of fear, but of power and of love and of a sound mind.

2.

"Every spirit of fear, worry, depression and panic in my life, I bind all of you and cast you all into the abyss this moment, in the name of Jesus.

3.

"From today, I break every evil covenant that has brought fear, worry and depression into my life, in the name of Jesus.

4.

"I command every terror of the night and arrow of the day that has brought fear and worry into my life to stop and move from my environment, in the name of Jesus.

5.

"I command every human agent using the spirits of fear to terrify me in the night to stumble and fall, in the name of Jesus.

6.

"The fear, terror and arrows of the doubters and the world, shall not be my portion, in the name of Jesus.

7.

"My tomorrow is blessed is Christ Jesus, My future is secure and guaranteed. Therefore, you spirit that is responsible for the fear and worry of tomorrow in my life, I bind you, in the name of Jesus.

8.

"Because my destiny is attached to God, therefore I decree that I can never fail, in the name of Jesus.

9.

"From this day, O LORD, I command every bondage I have subjected myself due to fear, worry and depression to be broken in Jesus name.

10.

"All negative doors that the spirit of fear, worry and depression has opened in in my life and family, be closed right now, in the name of Jesus Christ.

11.

"Every disease, oppression and hopelessness that came into my life as a result of fear and worry, disappear this moment, in the name of Jesus.

12.

"Every evil seed that has been planted into my life and family, as a result of fear, worry and panic, I command them to be uprooted this day, in Jesus name.

13.

"I refuse to be intimidated by any demonic nightmare from today. Let all the agents of darkness that appear in my dream to torment me disappear from now onwards in Jesus name.

14.

"I decree from today that I shall sleep and sleep in peace and wake up with joy and peace all around me, in Jesus name.

15.

"Every enchantment and invocation of fear and worry being made against me, I neutralize you, and I command you to fail, in the name of Jesus.

16.

"Every alliance of the enemies in my home with the enemies outside shall not stand, in the name of Jesus.

17.

"I destroy all efforts of the enemy to frustrate my work, in the name of Jesus.

18.

"I nullify every writing, agreement or covenant against my work, in the name of Jesus.

19.

"Father LORD, increase my greatness and comfort me on every side, in the name of Jesus.

20.

"O LORD, it is written that You delight in my prosperity. Therefore LORD, I pray that You bless me indeed in my work. Let no household enemy be able to control my well-being any longer, in the name of Jesus.

22.

"Let all those who are against me without a cause in my place of work turn back and be brought to confusion, in the name of Jesus.

23.

"My life is hid with Christ in God, therefore nobody can kill me or harm me. No weapon of Satan and his agents fashioned against me shall prosper, in the name of Jesus.

24.

"I command all doors leading to my blessings, victory and breakthroughs which the enemies have closed before now, to be OPENED WIDE from *today, in the name of Jesus.*

25.

"Every territorial spirit working against us in our neighborhood, be frustrated, bound and cast out into the abyss this day, in the name of Jesus Christ.

26.

"O LORD my Father, arrest, humiliate and neutralize every power contrary to Your name, operating in my house, environment and neighborhood, in the name of Jesus.

27.

"I bind every spirit of worry, fear, frustration and defeat operating in my house and family. I cast them into abyss in Jesus name.

28.

"I bind the spirit of death, armed robbery, burglary, terror and assassination in my neighborhood, in the name of Jesus Christ.

29.

"I reject, renounce and destroy every evil agreement or covenant working against my family and this neighborhood, in the name of Jesus.

30.

"By the blood of Jesus, I nullify the effects and operation of evil forces around my house, in the name of Jesus.

31.

"O LORD, let all my stubborn pursuers be occupied with unprofitable assignments, in the name of Jesus.

32.

"O LORD, expose and reveal the secrets of all my enemies masquerading as my friends, in Jesus name.

33.

Thank YOU LORD for my total deliverance. I am free from fear, worry, depression and panic attacks.

Let YOUR name be praised for ever and ever in my life, in Jesus name.

More Resources from Better Life World Outreach Center.

Please find below other materials published by Better Life World Outreach Centre. They are meant to be a blessing to your life and family.

1. Healing Prayers: 30 Powerful Prophetic Prayers that Brings Healing and Empower You to Walk in Divine Health.

2. Healing WORDS: 55 Powerful Daily Confessions & Declarations to Activate Your Healing & Walk in Divine Health: Strong Decrees That Invoke Healing for You & Your Loved Ones

3. Prayers That Break Curses and Spells and Release Favors and Breakthroughs.

4. 7 Days Fasting With 120 Powerful Night Prayers for Personal Deliverance and Breakthrough.

5. 100 Powerful Prayers for Teenagers

6. How to Pray for Your Family: + 70 Powerful Prayers and

Prophetic Declarations for Your Family's Salvation, Healing, Victory, Breakthrough & Total Restoration.

7. Daily Prayer Guide: A Practical Guide to Praying and Getting Results – Learn How to Develop a Powerful Personal Prayer Life

8. Make Him Respect You: 31 Relationship Advice for Women to Make their Men Respect Them.

9. How to Cleanse Your Home and Property from Demonic Attacks

Let's Connect.

Once again, thank you for reading this book. I believe you have been blessed.

Please consider giving it a review on Amazon. Your comment is very important to us.

Click Here to Write a Review about this book

We've also got other books on amazon. Take a look and be blessed:

www.amazon.com/author/danielokpara.

I also invite you to checkout our website at www.BetterLifeWorld.org and consider joining our newsletter, which we send out once in a while with great tips, testimonies and revelations from God's Word for a victorious living.

Feel free to drop us your prayer request. We will join faith with you and God's power will be released in your life and the issue in question.

We'd be very happy if you can share this book with others.

Remain blessed.

About the Author.

Daniel Okpara is an evangelist and teacher of God's Word whose ministry impacts hundreds of people each month via the Better Life Crusades, Better Life Health and Business Breakthrough Seminars and Better Life TV.

He is the international director of Better Life World Outreach Center, a non-denominational, evangelism based ministry with commitment to:

- Taking the entire Gospel to the entire world, from village to village, town to town, city to city, state to state and nation to nation, in partnership with established churches.
- Training ministers, evangelists and missionaries and providing them with tools,

resources and impartation for the end-time assignment.

- Restoring the evangelism fire in the body of Christ through church workers' revivals and trainings.
- Producing evangelism materials and tools (films, tracts, books, devotionals) for rural, screen and world evangelism.

He is the host of Better Life Today, a Monthly non-denominational fellowship meeting where hundreds of people gather for business workshops, worship, healing, miracles and diverse encounters with God. He also co-hosts a popular radio and TV program, **"Keys to a Better Life"**, aired in over 10 radio and TV stations across the country.

Daniel Okpara holds a Master's Degree in Theology

from Cornerstone Christian University. As a strong believer in hard work, continuous learning and prosperity by value creation, he is also the founder of Integrity Assets Ltd, a real estate and IT consulting company that manages an eCommerce startup and consults for companies on Digital Marketing.

He has authored over 50 books and manuals on healing, prayer, Marriage and relationship, Investment and business.

He is married to Prophetess Doris Okpara, a prayer warrior and great support and they are blessed with a boy and a girl, Isaac and Annabel.

Printed in Great Britain
by Amazon